關懷寬先生雅正
氣

JOURNEY INTO THE BODY, MIND, AND SOUL

An anthology on the ancient Chinese practice of cultivating Qi

Illustration on inside page, Wang Hehe (王赫赫) Chinese Calligraphy, 'Qi' 2007.

Cover Art, "Den Haag" by Christina Wollesen

Dedicated to my dearest mother and my family.

Also, to my most respectable Sifus for their enlightenment, precious skills, and lessons that they have bestowed upon me throughout my endless journey into the body, mind, and soul. Without them, I would not be who I am today, and for that, a simple thank you would never be enough.

ACKNOWLEDGEMENTS

I would like to thank my beloved daughter, Kristi. This book would not be a reality without her tremendous support and the numerous hours she spent editing these chapters and providing me with constructive suggestions and valuable comments. I must also extend a special thank you to my very dedicated and devoted student, Christina Wollesen, for her wholehearted support and commitment in designing the cover and overall layout of this book. Her enthusiasm, hard work, and dedication in the arrangements leading to the publication of this book have made this dream of mine possible.

The cover art of this anthology is a painting called "Den Haag," given to me by Christina as a gift. She is such a talented artist and I feel very proud to be able to guide her in her personal journey of Qigong training. I was truly touched when she presented me with her most treasured painting. For me, it evokes the feeling of peacefulness, which truly reflects the spirit of this book. Please, if you have the chance, take the time to explore more of her artwork.

In addition, I would like to express my sincerest thanks to my students Christina, Leon Ng, and Sue Lee for contributing their unique stories. I owe a special thanks to Leon who took the time to edit and touch up the images in this book.

PREFACE

The main purpose of publishing this book is not to prove the existence of Qi energy. It is not my intention to persuade readers to believe in or to follow what I have dedicated my life towards. However, the compilation of an anthology with an assortment of different articles serves as a true reflection of my personal experiences on my journey into the body, mind, and soul. For the past 30 years, I have trained extremely hard and I would like to share the fruits of my labour with those who are interested in (or simply curious about) the cultivation of Qi. I, of course, am a strong proponent of Qigong and its healing properties. Hence, this anthology is a testimony to my life's work in Qigong training. Some of these articles have been translated from my Chinese book "The Relationship of Tai Chi and Qi Emission" ("太極拳與布氣之妙合"), published in January of 2009 in Hong Kong. A few of my students have also enthusiastically contributed articles that discuss their encounters with Qi. I must give them appropriate credit for their eagerness and dedication towards this project. I truly value their stories and reflections, as they reveal a different perspective and fresh point of view. It is my hope to make my story accessible to a wider audience and that is why I embarked on this endeavour to publish a book in English.

A note must be made on the terminology and nomenclature mentioned in this book. I have done my best to translate Chinese terms to English. There are paragraphs (such as the one at the end of the introduction) dedicated to explaining terminology throughout this anthology; so rest assured that any questions relating to specific terms will likely be answered — should you choose to read on.

It is also important to mention that despite learning from one of the top Grandmasters in Chinese martial arts, I do not consider myself a martial artist. Nonetheless, it was my affinity for learning which led me onto a mysterious path towards Qi. The martial arts have undoubtedly played an essential role in my journey and have consequently become a critical part of my story. It was by chance that I stumbled upon Qigong, but perhaps, the mechanisms of fate were at work. Originally, I never once sought to enter the world of Qi. With time, however, I witnessed the power of Qi energy and was left with no choice but to believe.

This bark is rough,
and this body solid--
unmoving
like midnight waters.

Calm
as if cascading moonlight
bouncing across a seamless mirror
is no calamity at all

inhale, hold
just before jumping
from lily pad
to lily pad:
the apprehension is frozen,
but not still.

Not like the graceful giant
that pulls you in
with cold mountain air,
But akin to the permafrost
laying the foundation for life;
sustaining something that, ironically,
is not so permanent at all.

by its foot or by its roots
you can still see the clouds
even through the thick walls
of the ethereal mind

Within us, there beats a steady rhythm;
pulsing slow
but with potency.
Though unmoving
there is life coursing through my veins.

I am drawing breaths from the earth
up through the capillaries
of my steady core
And finally, through my branches
before vanishing
into thin air.

xylem, you are silent
but are you still?
I am listening to the forest thaw.

-- Kristi Kwan

CONTENTS

PART ONE

AFFINITY FOR LEARNING

INTRODUCTION

I have been practicing traditional Tai Chi, Qigong, Neigong, and other internal Chinese martial arts for over 30 years. My journey began in 1984, when I started studying traditional Yang style Tai Chi and Qigong under Sifu Y.C. Chan (陳英燦) in Hong Kong. He was a student of the late Grandmaster Yang Sau Chung (楊守中) of the Yang family Tai Chi and he taught me for about 4 years. Later in Canada, I met one of the top Grandmasters in Chinese martial arts, Pan Qing Fu (潘清福師父). He was the senior chief coach of the Chinese National Martial Arts Delegation as well as the Tianjin, Hunan, and Liaoning provinces' professional martial arts teams. He was also the chief instructor of self-defense for the Chinese Police and Special Forces. Pan Qing Fu captured a total of 23 gang leaders during the Cultural Revolution in China, earning his fame as a relentless gang-buster– but that's another story we will visit later on. In addition, he acted in and choreographed movies such as "Shaolin Temple" (1982) starring Jet Li, "Iron & Silk" (1990) starring Mark Salzman, "Talons of the Eagle" (1992) starring Billy

Blank, and "Last to surrender" (1999). In 1990, I became his first formal disciple in Canada.

Although Grandmaster Pan is famous for his Iron Fist, Iron Stomach, Eagle Claw, and other external martial arts, my heart was set on Tai Chi. I began with Tai Chi training, but naturally, as a disciple of Grandmaster Pan, I was also involved with weapons training. Of course, this was no surprise given my Sifu's (師父) reputation as one of the top fighters in mainland China. I became skilled with the Long Sword, Pa Kua Broadsword, and in White Wax Long-pole (Dai Gan) power training. I learned Chin Na (Joint Lock Technique) together with other self-defense techniques. I was also trained in a variety of other internal martial arts such as Hsing Yi and Pa Kua. Despite the diversity of my training, I knew I had my own path. I did not want to deviate from my journey in Tai Chi. For me, there was no pressure to become like my Sifu. I did not want to be a good fighter and it was not my calling to become like him. External martial arts were not for me because I needed to keep my movements soft, yet powerful. In my view, Tai Chi is much like a song; music that can be both gentle and potent.

Many martial artists think that training in mixed martial arts such as Karate, Wrestling, Kick-boxing, Kung Fu, or other hard external styles will help them when practising

Tai Chi, but I completely disagree. I view the experience of hard martial arts as a burden, since it prevents many people from being totally relaxed. It is extremely difficult to relax every muscle in your body if you have been practicing hard styles. With this view, I tried to avoid having that baggage in my training. The core principle in Tai Chi

With Sifu Pan in 1990, following the disciple ceremony

is relaxation of both the mind and the physical movements. This is the most important criterion.

Perhaps in an unusual twist of fate, I later met another Qigong master, Tai Yeen Wong (汪棣賢師父). One day in 1997, I received a package from Hong Kong. I found a book together with a handwritten note inside. It was sent to me by my childhood friend and neighbour. We had lost contact for over a decade, so this came to me as a big surprise. He suggested that I visit his teacher, who had immigrated to Canada recently. My friend mentioned that Master Wong was extremely skilled in Qigong, Qi projection, and Wu style Tai Chi. After reading Tai Yeen Wong's book, I thought it would be worthwhile to reach out to him. There was one specific type of Neigong that I really wanted to learn and it turns out that Master Wong is one of few masters who has knowledge about the details. This style of Neigong originated from the Wu family school of Tai Chi.

Upon meeting Master Wong, I knew that his coming to Canada was a golden opportunity for learning. Despite the visit being our very first encounter, the feeling was familiar and the conversation flowed easily. I was extremely surprised when he immediately agreed to teach me privately. In this way, I started my new journey into Qigong and Wu Tai Chi. I studied with Master Wong for about 10 years. He is the gatekeeper of Sui Yuan Qigong, as well as an Indoor disciple of the late Wu Tai Chi (吳大齊) (1926-1993). Wu Tai Chi was a fourth generation Grandmaster of the Wu's family Tai Chi.[1] I was first accepted by Master Wong as his disciple in 1999 and was eventually chosen as one of his Indoor disciples in 2007. To this day, I continue to visit him in Hong Kong whenever I have the chance. Over the years, even oceans apart, we have managed to maintain our strong bond. We have never lost contact and I always follow his words and incorporate what he has taught me in my daily practice.

In Chinese martial arts, Tai Chi, Qigong or other traditional arts such as herbal medicine, Beijing and Cantonese opera, or even painting and calligraphy, there is a distinction between a *student,* and a *disciple.* In general, there is no serious commitment between a student and a teacher; only a general and mutual responsibility of teaching and learning exists. On the other hand, a disciple is expected to seriously devote themselves to the master, and the art of the master. The disciple must be committed to master a unique and secret inner branch of knowledge. The relationship between a disciple and a master is very sacred and the obligations and responsibilities are binding. The duties

1 Chen, Yang, Wu, Hao and Sun are the traditional Tai Chi families originally. Most of their secretive skills are still only passed down to family members and selected disciples.

of a disciple reflect their strong bond with the master. Obligations are severe and any form of betrayal comes with grave consequences. Moreover, the word "Sifu" (師父) in Chinese is literally the combination of teacher "師" and father "父". In some cases, some masters may choose to select and accept special or beloved disciples as their "Indoor Disciples" (入室弟子). This is especially the case for the gatekeepers of the family (the ones who carry on the torch). Normally, only "Indoor Disciples" are allowed to teach the art of the master. Subsequently, they receive more guidance and are given the opportunity to learn more and delve deeper into the art than regular disciples.

My Sifus have been very influential in my lifelong journey of training. Though my teaching style may not mirror those of my Sifus, important core principles they have taught me are held very dear to my heart. In teaching my own students, these values certainly shine through.

With Sifu Wong in 2007, following the indoor disciple ceremony

IRON FIST – A TALE FROM THE CULTURAL REVOLUTION

Upon first glance at my Sifu, Grandmaster Pan, the exceptionally thick calluses on his right knuckles will undoubtedly attract your attention. The biggest callus is on his third knuckle…and it is about half an inch thick. These calluses are rough in surface and hard as steel, but the rest of his hand looks perfectly smooth and soft. I remember one time I was with my Sifu at a drug store. The clerk was a warmhearted old lady (albeit a little naïve) who recommended some medication to fix his calluses. She must have thought that he had some serious skin problems after catching a glimpse of his hand. She did not understand that these tremendously thick calluses, though seemingly terrifying to many, were the spectacular result of years of dedicated training and discipline.

Grandmaster Pan is considered a world-renowned expert in Iron Fist training. Born in a relatively poor village in the Shandong province of China, he began such training when he was just a young boy. At that time, it was very popular for boys to engage in street fighting. However, their form of "fist fighting" was not actual fighting. Instead, the boys would hit each other's fists knuckle to knuckle. If one succumbed to the pain and ran away, the other would automatically become the winner. He said to

Sifu Pan demonstrates his Iron Fist training, 1993

me, "If your fist is hard and strong, with both power and speed, you can defend yourself. If your fist is soft and weak, your power will in turn, hurt your own fist."

And so, since a very young age, my Sifu developed a habit of tapping and punching a steel block over a thousand times each day as part of his training routine. He always said to me, "One punch is better than saying a thousand words." According to Grandmaster Pan, punching steel strengthens and conditions the bone and surrounding tissue. The theory behind this is that the composition of steel is very dense and the force of the punch will resonate back into the fist (thereby increasing the strength and density of the bone). Grandmaster Pan suggests that students begin with softer materials such as sand bags, wood, or a smooth concrete block. Gradually switching to much denser materials (such as steel) and increasing the power of your punch over a long period of time will yield the best results.

"Everything feels soft after punching steel for a period of time," he would say with a smile. He further emphasized that one should train under a qualified master of Iron Fist. If trained incorrectly, one could incur serious injuries and permanently damage the joints of the hand.

In addition to teachings on martial arts, my Sifu often told me tales of his life. There was one incident he described that I remember especially clearly. This story took place during the Cultural Revolution in China (1966-1976), which was initiated by Mao Zedong, Chairman of the Communist Party of China. Its goal was to purge the opposition forces within the party itself, so that orthodox communism could be enforced in the country and society as a whole. Mao criticized government officials, claiming that bourgeois liberalism was infiltrating the government and society in an attempt to restore capitalism. He insisted that any revisionists should be removed through violent class struggle. His voice was echoed by many Chinese youth who supported his choice to eliminate any traces of capitalism, even if it meant using violence and physical force. Soon, Red Guard cult groups formed around the country. As a result, it led to massive conflicts and large-scale class struggles filled with violence and bloodshed. Millions of citizens and party officials were persecuted and abused. They suffered attacks and were subjected to kidnappings, confiscation of personal property, imprisonment, torture, execution, and public humiliation. The movement even spread to the military and local police and security forces. In an attempt to control the chaos, the government had banned all firearms possession by citizens, including the police.

This created a window of opportunity for many gangsters to commit serious crimes throughout the country. At the request of the local police chief in Shenyang (a city in the Liaoning province), Grandmaster Pan accepted the mission to assist the police in locating and capturing gang leaders. It wasn't long before his victories against many hard-core criminals earned him fame as a local hero. He single-handedly captured a total of 23 gang leaders. The most captivating tale he told was one that took place at a local eatery.

One day, he spotted one of the most wanted fugitives at a restaurant. It was around lunch hour at the time and the restaurant was very crowded, packed with many customers. My Sifu immediately tried to capture the fugitive, but was met with a sudden kick aimed at his groin. The bad guy was about 6 feet tall and weighed over 200 lbs with a very strong and muscular build. He tried to wrestle my Sifu to the ground by using Shuai Jiao (wrestling) techniques. At 5'7" and weighing about 135 lbs, the odds seemed stacked against my Sifu.

After a couple of lightning-fast moves, Grandmaster Pan ducked to the side and returned him with a punch to the face. His opponent's face was so swollen that it had grown to twice its original size. Despite receiving such a powerful blow to the head, he was still standing – swaying, but not fallen. My Sifu needed to deliver another punch to finish the job. Even years later, he gets very upset when telling this story, repeating how he could not stop blaming himself for the rest of his life. This was what my Sifu saw as the *regret of a lifetime*: not having finished his opponent off with just a single punch.

THE LONG SWORD

The first time I saw a performance of the "Long Sword" was in the movie "Iron & Silk." It was performed by my Sifu, Grandmaster Pan Qing Fu, together with his student, Mark Salzman. The movie was based on the true story of English teacher, Mark Salzman, and takes place in the late 1980s when he was teaching English in Hunan, China. At the time, my Sifu was the head coach of the Hunan province's professional martial arts team and agreed to take Salzman as his student. Both Mark Salzman and my Sifu play themselves in the movie.

It was the unique shape of the Long Sword that fascinated me and soon, I became obsessed with the idea of learning it. One day in 1991, during a training session with my Sifu, I finally had the courage to ask if he would teach me. However, my request was turned down immediately. He sternly expressed that he would never teach anybody. Before I had the chance to ask about Salzman, he told me that he only taught Salzman a few of the basic movements with the Long Sword for the movie. Of course, I was disappointed, but I said to myself that he probably had a valid reason for not teaching this specific weapons training. To this day, I hold the highest respect for my Sifu. I believe that as a disciple or student, it is crucial to trust and have complete faith in your Sifu or teacher. It is important to trust in their wisdom and to understand that if your Sifu makes a decision you do not understand or agree with, he or she must have their reasons.

Later on, I discovered more details about this weapon. My Sifu told me that Japanese Kendo originated from the Long Sword. It was originally transferred from China to Korea, and later to Japan many centuries ago. The Japanese learned some basic skills from the Long Sword and later adapted them until they became their own techniques in Kendo.

I thought I would never get the chance to learn how to wield the Long Sword from my Sifu. However, one day in 1997, he told me that I would soon need to move to a bigger house. I didn't understand what he meant by that. With a mischievous glint in his eyes, he explained that my house was not big enough for the training of the Long Sword. Still in shock, but pleasantly surprised, I asked him why he changed his mind and eventually decided to teach me. His answer was this: "There is only one Kelly Kwan in this world." He continued to reflect: "None of my formal Sifus [a total of 15] were purposely trying to *not* teach me the secret techniques. It did not depend on them. It depended on whether or not you could impress the gods."

With that, my Sifu finally agreed to teach me his most treasured weapons training after about 8 years of a 'fa-

Training with the Long Sword, 1998

ther-son like relationship'. My commitment was true, and upon reflection, I had made some very real sacrifices in order to put my Sifu first. He always said to me, "A student must travel a thousand miles to find a good master, but if a master were to look for a good and loyal disciple, it would take even more than ten thousand miles."

It is no surprise that many traditional masters are quite hesitant to teach their secret skills openly to their students in the first couple of years. Normally, disciples are put under strict observation during a probationary period, which lasts for a long time before they really receive any direct training from the master. Only disciples who are pure of heart are deemed worthy of being taught these techniques. Of course, they must also have an extremely good relationship with their master in order to earn the privilege to learn the truly secret skills.

My Sifu always said to me: "Even a tough guy needs three good helpers" ("一個好漢三個幫"). He meant that even the strongest person needs help from others in their daily life. I remember helping my Sifu obtain a U.S. visa more than twenty years ago. He desperately needed a visa in order to attend the movie premiere of "Iron & Silk" in New York City.

The U.S. authority requested that he have a valid visitor's visa since he was only a landed immigrant in Canada, still holding a Chinese passport. At that time in 1991, all applicants needed to line-up in front of the U.S. Embassy in order to obtain a number before they could be allowed into the office. However, there was a daily quota with regards to the number of applicants they processed each day. I remember the first day I went; the weather was bitter and cold with a wind chill around -25°C. I arrived at 6:30 in the morning, just to find approximately 150 people lined-up before me. I waited until 8 o'clock when they announced that the quota was already full for the day. I left empty-handed, but resolved to return the next day.

The second time around, I planned to go much earlier. I lined up at 5 o'clock, before the crack of dawn. It was freezing cold and many people were hiding in their sleeping bags. However, I had nothing and was left with no choice but to stand there for three hours without any shelter. My hands, feet, and face all seemed frozen to the point where I could hardly move. At 8 o'clock, I finally got a number. I held it in my frost-bitten hands as I spotted my Sifu arriving with another student. I thought for sure this time we would not have any problems getting a visa. To my complete and utter dismay, we were told that the Embassy needed other documents to finalize my Sifu's application. That meant only one thing: I needed to return and get a number again the next day. When I got home, I told my wife about the whole ordeal. Appalled, she stared and said, in a very serious tone, "Would you do the same thing for your own father?"

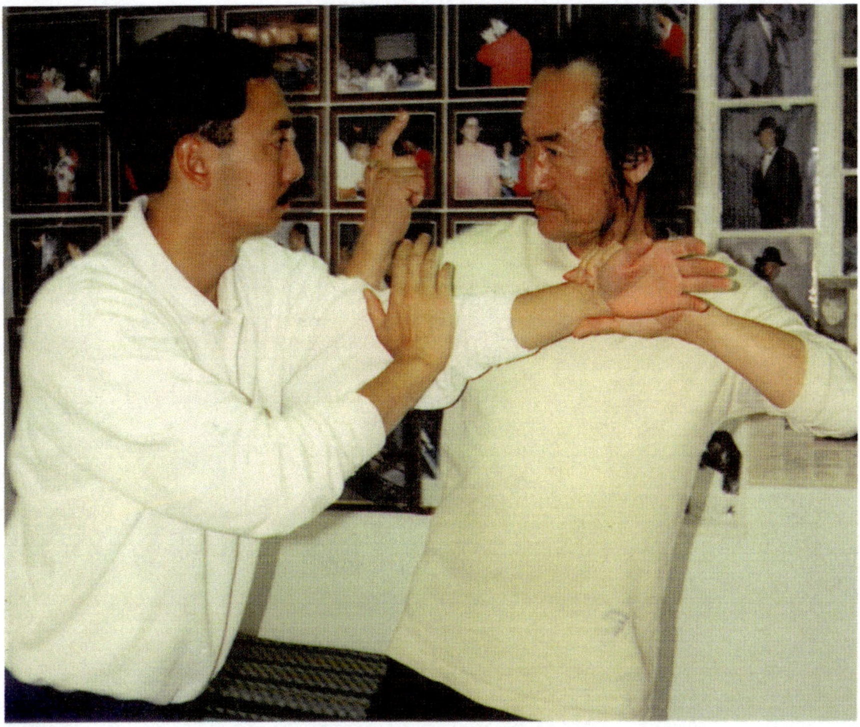

Training in Push Hands with Sifu Pan, 1992

MISSION POSSIBLE

"Martial Arts training without stretching and kicking diminishes the ability and effectiveness of movement when one ages."

- Grandmaster Pan Qing Fu

Stretching increases flexibility, mobility, strength, and balance. This is absolutely true for all kinds of martial arts training including internal styles such as Tai Chi, Hsing Yi, and Pa Kua. Many martial arts practitioners, however, ignore the importance of stretching. Some achieved good flexibility when they were young, but often lose it simply due to lack of perseverance in stretching over the years.

In my experience, stretching is an invaluable part of martial arts training that brings tremendous benefits. I have been practicing Tai Chi, Qigong, and other styles of martial arts since my mid-20s. I remember my first Tai Chi teacher only taught me the forms without even mentioning the importance of stretching. I learned the full set of Yang Style Tai Chi movements in about eight months, yet I advanced very little despite training for 3 to 4 hours each day. My stance was comparatively high and narrow, and I encountered difficulties while executing some kicking and balancing movements. In spite of this, I thought my training in Tai Chi was sufficient and complete. I practiced the routines everyday without any interruption for a couple of years. In retrospect, I realize I was completely overlooking the importance of stretching. In fact, I only spent a few minutes on some warm-up exercises before I began

High kick with toes touching forehead

practicing Tai Chi and other routines.

Most people would probably agree that Tai Chi is the most popular and widely practiced martial art. Many Tai Chi practitioners, though, overemphasize the form (the movements themselves) and fail to stress the necessity of stretching. Most of us believe that the movements of Tai Chi include gentle stretching of the joints and muscles, which ultimately leads to greater flexibility. This is only true to some extent. Some movements in Tai Chi actually require a greater degree of flexibility, and cannot be performed with just an average range of motion. For example, the Single Whip Squat and Lotus Kick both involve a high degree of flexibility in the hip and leg. In the Single Whip Squat, one needs to sit very low on the right foot while stretching the left foot straight, having it almost touch the ground.

My concept of stretching changed dramatically after I met my first Sifu, Grandmaster Pan Qing Fu. I became his disciple in 1990, and this began my journey anew. I clearly remember the first time my Sifu commented on my Tai Chi movements. He told me that all my movements were "empty." That is, not reflecting their practical application in fighting. He told me to start from zero if I wanted to improve my skills. This was quite a shock to me. I had been practicing for seven consecutive years. It is no easy task for one to give up all that one has learned. It was a very painful decision indeed.

I eventually accepted his suggestion and started learning from the beginning again. My Sifu always lectured me about the importance of stretching in martial arts training. This, for me, shaped a brand new concept of stretching. At first, I thought it would be too late for me to engage in any serious stretching, as I was 31-years-old at the time. I had met a gymnastics coach from China who used to be the head coach for the Shanghai gymnastics team. He told me that it would be nearly impossible for me to achieve the full splits at my age. This comment ignited something within me. Perhaps I took it as a challenge, but I began to dream of doing the splits.

Single Whip Squat

I later told Sifu Pan about this during a training session at his home in 1991, and his answer was this:
"Disregard what he told you. Most people with average standards or average expectations will only come up with mediocre or average opinions. If you want to be outstanding in martial arts, you should not be afraid of any obstacles or difficulties, such as age or physical limitations. Challenge leads to improvement. If you can "eat bitter" [endure hardship], *you will succeed eventually."*

He explained further that stretching is an advanced technique which requires special training. If you stretch only as a warm-up exercise, you will never be flexible. Stretching is what he regards as "self-inflicted pain," but gradually it would lead to greater flexibility. Till this day, my Sifu's favorite saying is "No pain, no gain."

From then on, I began to stretch under his guidance. I spent about two hours daily, just on stretching. I developed a large bruise around the back of both my knees after the first week of intensive stretching. I even had to carry a hot water bottle with me to work, in order to relieve the pain. I was repeatedly warned by my family about possibly damaging my legs for good. Gradually, after a month of continuous stretching, I began to feel better. Progress was slow, but after persevering for approximately two years, I was able to kick higher than before. I could significantly extend my stance. Most of all, I could also do a full split with ease on the ground or atop two chairs (one under each foot, resulting in a split in mid-air). Furthermore, I could deliver a high front kick and pull that foot with both hands inwards to touch my forehead. As my kicking leg is longer than my upper body, this was quite a difficult feat. I needed to bend my knee in the opposite direction in order for my toes to touch my forehead.

Sifu Pan told me that the best benefit from stretching is that your body remains young and your confidence grows with age. Most importantly, though (from a martial arts point of view), your legs will move faster and gain more power to strengthen your kicking ability. In addition, you will be able to move quickly from one stance to another with increased force, agility, and control. He added that

Different kinds of stretching

the front stretch is the most important, as well as the most difficult. If you improve this stretch, you will tread lighter and the length of your stride will increase. You would even see a difference in your walk!

In time, I got a chance to show these movements to the gymnastics coach I had mentioned earlier. Impressed, he admired my flexibility. He responded that he hadn't meant that I could not perform the splits at my age, but rather, that most people simply could not 'stretch open their mind.' "Their mind," he said, "is preoccupied with the notion that this kind of flexibility is impossible to achieve due to their advancing age."

In conclusion, people generally have misconceptions about their potential to achieve great physical flexibility. I am living proof that regardless of age and in spite of other limitations one may live with, it can be done. The wide misconception also extends to the vital role that flexibility plays in improving one's ability in almost all areas of martial arts practice – indeed, in laying and in maintaining the foundations for a solid and effective core technique. I would like to urge those of you reading this to incorporate stretching into your daily practice as much as possible; make it as important as form, speed, fluidity, and focus. Your perspective on your practice and your body will dramatically change.

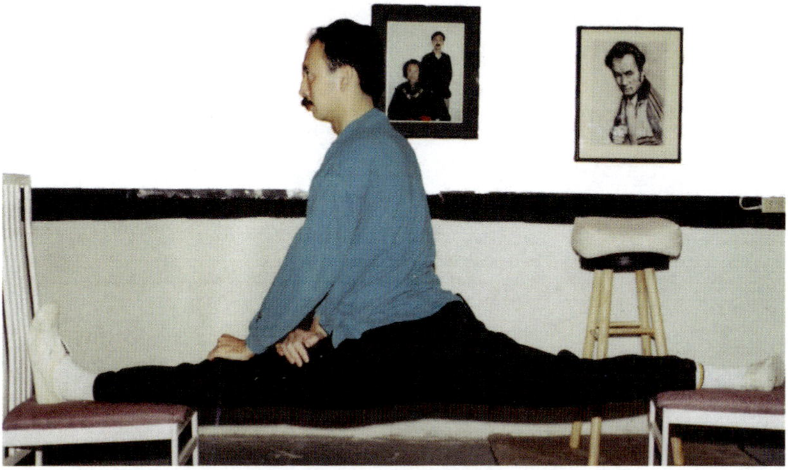

Doing the splits with legs balanced on two chairs

他媽的 (DAMN IT!), BY LEON NG

"他媽的! (Damn it!) … Too tense! …Relax! Relax!..."

To the public those words are meaningless. To me they mean a lot since they come from my 師父 (Sifu) Kelly Kwan. It is the essence of and main criterion for the Internal Arts.

The world of Martial Arts, either in fantasy or culture, has always been a part of my childhood. I owe credit to my mother who was an avid fantasy reader, TV addict, and worried parent. She saw value in instilling manners and cultures for her children. More importantly, she wanted us to have the skill of self-defense to protect ourselves from the harsh, cruel world of reality. It was through her that I had the opportunity to become a student of 師父. Thus, the seeds of fate were sown.

My life journey in martial arts would be split into two phases. My induction into traditional Chinese martial arts began with the foundations, focusing on forms and applications. The old school training was not for the faint of heart. For example, learning to do the splits meant being manually pulled with pressure applied to the legs in both directions. Weight training, meant carrying bricks while walking in circles. Iron arm training was performed by hitting a tree to toughen the muscles and bones. The focus was to transform external energy into internal energy by subjecting the physical body to rigorous practice and drills. The idea of Qi was rarely mentioned and if mentioned, it was brief.

Reflecting on these initial years of training, I was working my muscles and limbs while there was a feeling of emptiness inside the body– like I was lacking substance. I experimented with other martial arts such as Karate and Judo to null the feeling. The experiment produced the same end result: something was missing internally. Some would suggest a lack of faith leading to an absence of peace within oneself. But I was sure that the emptiness was not because I lacked faith or religion. The feeling of vulnerability stemmed from within the organs themselves. The other possibility would have been that internal energy had not yet developed in my body. If this was the case, then it would surely lead to questions of self-doubt. My entire goal in training was to develop internal energy. I began to wonder: Was my training all focused only on external energy? Was my pursuit of internal energy for nothing? Did I deviate from training instructions? Was I putting enough hours in training? Was it the machinations of fate at work?

As time passes, God likes to make life interesting. I departed from my training to focus on other commitments in life (i.e. studies and establishing a career). In the following years, time was very kind to me. I made some intimate friends that would soon be permanent…他媽的! (Damn it!). My loyal friends often showed up at the most important moments in my life. To name a few:

- Pain of the Right Knee– caused by inflammation of the ligament (I suspect Gout);
- Irregular Heart Rate (Arrhythmia)– caused by stress from modern society;
- Tense shoulders – caused by chronic repeated action and stress;
- Cracked molar (vertical crack) coupled with receding gums that caused pain when chewing;
- Feelings of coldness in the body even when wearing a Canada goose jacket in warm weather;

Western physicians diagnosed my symptoms. All doctors would offer me a drug along with the age-old statement: "We shall monitor the condition." A permanent solution could never be found. Disheartened by the outcome, I decided to take charge of my own life. It began with a lifestyle change: eating healthier, increasing exercise, taking supplements and vitamins, and using environmentally friendly products (to reduce the number of chemicals I was exposed to in my household). I could tell that these changes helped to subtly alleviate the pain, but they failed to completely resolve the persistent issues I was having.

Occasionally, I would go back to visit and catch up

with 師父. One particular visit sparked an interesting topic: Qi. He asked me if I believed in Qi. I hesitated in my reply to his question. He must have sensed my hesitation because he proceeded to demonstrate a few examples to state its existence. The first example, he showed me his palm. The center of the palm (Meridian point Lao Gong – Palace of Labour) would grow in size resembling a pea, while the rest of his hand remained the same. Another time, he asked Sue, his coworker, for assistance. He placed his hand over her head and within minutes, Sue began to involuntarily spin like a ballerina while she was still conscious and conversing with me. I was skeptical, but at that moment I was at a loss for words. Many questions flooded my mind: Was it a slight of hand? Was it physics? Was I hypnotized? It cannot easily be explained. I am aware that a fine line exists between insanity and greatness. I would like to think that I am a very logical person since I have a technical background in computers. The evidence was so convincing. I knew that if it were greatness, then 師父's art had ventured into another realm - the world of Qi. This was every martial artist's dream, one of higher enlightenment.

After a few more visits, 師父 noticed the decline in my health. Unreserved and honest, he said: "You look awful. You need to train more." He commented that my body had lost its shine. My presence was emitting an aura of dullness and fatigue. I assured him that I was still training daily at a reduced intensity due to time constraints. A few more visits later, he gave me an offer that I could not refuse. This would be the start of my journey into the world of Qi. We started with Qigong to rebuild my health, before revisiting the fundamentals of internal arts that I had missed and neglected. After months of training, I noticed some transformations in the body during and after the training process:

- Pain associated with my "intimate friends" had been greatly reduced or completely eliminated;
- Left hand – sensation of a hole in the center of my palm and air flowing through;
- A sensation of needles prickling the inside of my palm;
- A sensation of warmth dwelling inside my stomach;
- A sensation of warmth in my kidneys, and becoming conscious of their existence;
- A warm tingling feeling rushing from the base of the spine to the crown of my head;
- A sensation of a hole with leaking substance at the top of my scalp and a conscious pulsating feeling;
- Increased energy and stamina;
- The body, as a whole, is more relaxed; sensation of regaining youth from my late teen years.

Most of these sensations appear and disappear as they please. Is this a cruel joke from Qi? I do not know. Skeptics will state that an increase in blood circulation due to exercise could logically explain these symptoms of improvement. Equally possible is a psychological effect of the mind. I would challenge any skeptics out there to try and experience the same results from just any type of exercise. I am sure that these sensations will not result solely from regular exercise and weight training(e.g. push-ups, jogging, Pilates, etc.). Regardless of the controversy surrounding the existence of Qi, the end result is that I feel healthier.

Recently, I had the honour of experiencing Qi projection. As the test subject, I was instructed to stand fully relaxed with my eyes closed. 師父 placed his hand behind my back. Involuntarily, within 3 minutes, I felt my body performing a gymnastics bridge. I had no control over the position of my body. Sue, as our witness, was shocked to see the degree of bending in my back. It was as if I was a piece of paper being folded in half (a v-shaped bend). I felt an invisible energy tugging at my body. I was not hypnotized since I still had sensations and was fully aware of my surroundings. My natural reflex was to grasp the floor with my feet to stabilize my balance. The only explanation I can find is that Qi was at work. 師父 was able to generate an energy force and send it into my body. The human body is porous (e.g. sweat and liquids can leak through the skin) and hence, we are receptive to the environment. Qi energy from 師父 could provide a high level explanation for what had happened. Such energy triggered the suction or tugging within my body, causing it to bend backwards in half.

In conclusion, Fate took me on a road trip which I will never forget. It introduced me to the internal arts, despite a slight detour. Now, with my return to the internal arts, I am coming full circle. More importantly, I have found something that is effective in keeping my "intimate friends" at bay. I will not dwell on the concept of Qi. The best suggestion is to try it yourself rather than debate or criticize its existence. Take it for what it is worth. Do not complicate the topic. One must ask the question: Is there any harm in exploring it? Do you have anything to lose? Empty your cup, because your health is your wealth.

他媽的! (Damn it!) Talk is cheap, try it and enjoy the ride!

PART TWO

QI AND QIGONG

Qi energy is considered a vital life-force that exists in our bodies, living organisms, and the universe itself. Traditional Chinese medicine and Qigong practitioners have identified a wide range of Qi. Human beings are born with Yuan Qi (元氣), also known as "Real Qi" (真氣) or "Pre-Natal Qi" (先天氣). It is the Qi we have inherited from our parents and it is stored in our kidneys. However, this Qi needs to be nourished by the intake and absorption of nutrients such as food, water, and the fresh air in our environment. This latter Qi then becomes Hou Tian Qi (後天氣) or "Post-Natal Qi".

Pre-Natal Qi (Yuan Qi or Real Qi) flows through our whole body and internal organs. Qi that travels to different organs will have different names such as Stomach-Qi, Spleen-Qi, Kidney-Qi, Heart-Qi, Lung-Qi, and Liver-Qi. Qi also travels to different Meridian channels and becomes a specific type of Qi at that channel. From the Chinese medicinal point of view, the balance and smooth flow of Qi in your body, internal organs, and Meridian channels will result in good health and longevity. Imbalanced and stagnant Qi flow will lead to diseases.

According to Taoism, the two major fundamental forms of Qi are Yin-Qi (陰氣) and Yang-Qi (陽氣). They are considered primordially feminine and masculine energies, respectively. These two energies need to be in a balanced state in order for one to stay healthy, both physically and mentally. It is also believed that Qigong, together with diet, Chinese herbs, and a holistic lifestyle, contributes to balancing the Yin and Yang in our bodies.

Qigong practice is regarded as an effective way to promote good health by strengthening the human body, preventing diseases, and prolonging life. It includes two important aspects: (1) a psychosomatic self-training method, wherein the postures of the human body along with breathing are regulated while relaxing the mind; and (2) diligent Qigong training or external Qi projection in healing. Normally, Qigong practitioners attain the Xiao Zhou Tian (Small Circle) and Dai Zhou Tian (Big Circle) before they can really develop any ability in external Qi projection. Many studies in China and other countries indicate that a well-trained Qigong master can produce an exceptional level of biological electric and magnetic currents in the body while manipulating Qi.

SMALL CIRCLE AND BIG CIRCLE

I developed my ability in Qi emission after intensive practice and training for 21 years. In 2005, I finally attained a state of "smooth passage," which allows the Qi to travel through the Ren and Du Meridians (Small Circle, or Xiao Zhou Tian) and eventually through the twelve Meridian channels (Big Circle, or Dai Zhou Tian) as well.

Qigong is closely related to Meridian channels and acupoints. Advanced Qigong practitioners can feel Qi flow along the channels when their training reaches certain heightened levels. Some Qigong masters will even develop various degrees of supernatural power after passing through the Xiao Zhou Tian (Small Circle) and the Dai Zhou Tian (Big Circle). With the combination of the intent and imagination, they can project their internal Qi from certain points in their body for healing purposes.

SMALL CIRCLE (小周天)

Xiao Zhou Tian, or Small Circle, is the natural phenomenon in which Qi travels in a circular pathway from the Dantian (3 cun below the umbilicus) upward toward the Changqiang acupoint (a point between the tip of the coccyx and the anus)– provided that you can accumulate sufficient Qi in your Dantian through training. However, using strong intent without sufficient accumulation of Qi in your Dantian (and without proper guidance from a knowledgeable master) will, in many cases, lead to serious physical and mental implications. A diagram and table of the pathway and specific acupoints follows in this section (p.40-41). Most of the table has been taken from the "Body Model for Both Meridian and Extraordinary Points of China" (GB 12346-90). The measurement "cun" refers to the Chinese inch "寸," a traditional unit of length that is used to chart acupuncture points on the human body. Though there is debate, it is generally accepted that 1 cun is the width of one's thumb at the knuckle, 1.5 cun is the width of the two forefingers, and the total width of all fingers side-by-side is equal to 3 cun.

Xiao Zhou Tian Diagram

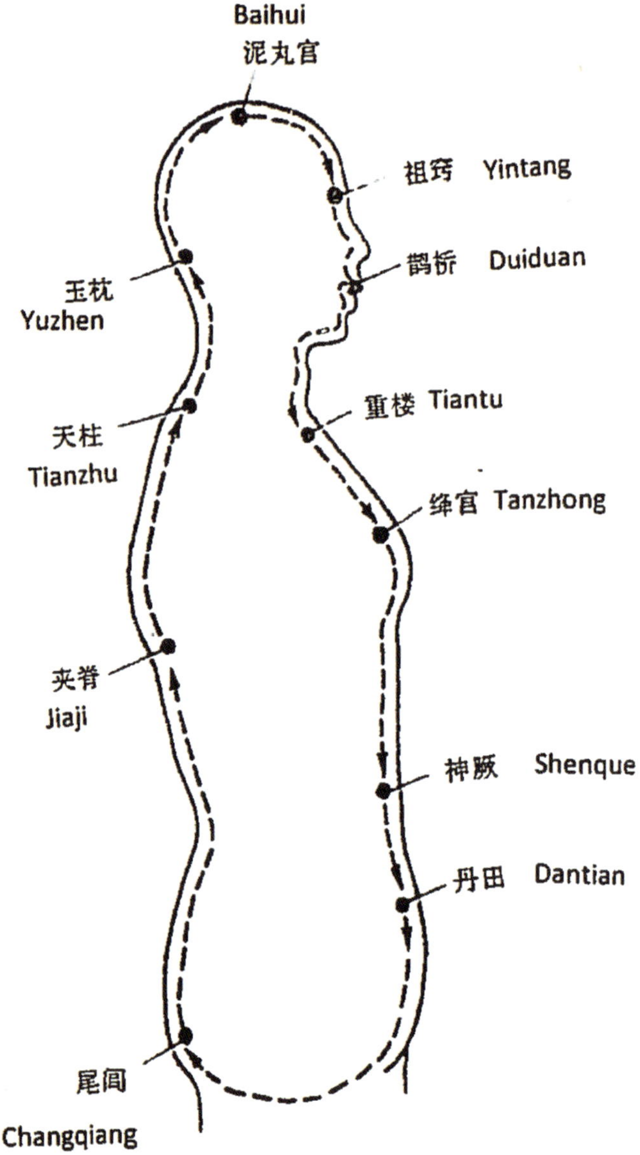

The pathway begins at the Dantian and moves toward the Changqiang. The Qi will further travel upward, reaching these acupoints in the following order (see diagram on opposite page, and table on p.42):

Jiaji – Tianzhu – Yuzhen – Baihui – Yintang

From the Yintang, the Qi moves downward through this path:

Suliao – Shuigou – Duiduan

Once the Qi reaches the Diuduan, this is the point where it connects with the Ren Meridian (Conception Vessel). The Ren Meridian travels from the Tiantu downward to the Lianquan (throat), and along the chest toward the Tanzhong. The Qi continues further down again, passing through the Shenque (belly button), Yinjiao, Qihai, Guanyuan, and Zhongji before completing the cycle at the Dantian.

Table 1.1: Xiao Zhou Tian (Small Circle) Major Acupoints

Changqiang	Between the tip of the coccyx and the anus
Jiaji	0.5 cun beside the lower border of each spinal process (from T1, the 1st thoracic vertebra, to L5, the 5th lumbar vertebra)
Tianzhu (Celestial Pillar)	Right on the natural hairline at the back of the head, on the lateral part of the margin of the trapezius muscle (1.3 cun lateral to the Ta-man; between the spinal processes of C7, the 7th cervical vertebra, and T1, the 1st thoracic vertebra)
Yuzhen (Jade Pillow)	On the lateral part of the upper margin of the external occipital protuberance and opposite the Tianzhu down below (1.3 cun lateral to Naohu - on the head, 2.5 cun above the mid-point of the posterior hairline)
Baihui (Hundred Convergences)	5 cun from the middle of the natural hair-line; 1.5 cun before Houting (1.5 cun before Chiangchien)
Yintang (Hall of Seal)	At the midpoint between the eyebrows
Suliao	At the centre of the nose apex
Duiduan	The tip of the philtrum (midpoint of the upper lip)
Tiantu	The middle of the depression above the su-prasternal notch (the mid-point between your lower lip and your jaw)
Tanzhong	Midway between the nipples and level with the 4th intercostal space
Shenque	Centre of the umbilicus

THREE FLOWERS CROWNING THE HEAD

According to my own experience, there will be some significant sensations and movements in the Dantian and surrounding areas while you accumulate sufficient Qi. At one point in my practice, I regularly felt strong contractions on my Huiyin (midway between the anus and the scrotum) and my testicles were spinning to the point where it seemed like they had been sucked upward, tightly against my body. I then felt a strong current moving upward slowly from my tail bone to the upper part of my back. This sensation came back repeatedly many times during my regular daily training for the next six months. Then one day, I experienced two mild bumping sensations on top of my head (like something was trying to burst out from my scalp). This was followed by the feeling of pins and needles at the crown of my head.

I was a bit worried at first and I did not know what to do. I talked to my Sifu, Master Wong, about my sensations. He told me that it is probably a condition called "Three Flowers Crowning the Head" ("三花貫頂"). His advice was that I should try and relax, and mildly tap my head whenever I felt discomfort. This sensation lasted for about three months until one day, again during my training, I felt a strong sensation of contractions on my Yintang (mid-point between the eyebrows) for a couple of minutes. I then felt something resembling the mist from a waterfall dripping gently down from my forehead. My tongue was sucked upward with the tip of my tongue touching my hard palate. I felt a lot of saliva dripping down my throat. I knew this was the beginning of the Xiao Zhou Tian journey.

For centuries, Xiao Zhou Tian has been the most desirable phenomenon for almost all Qigong (Tao and Zen) practitioners, holistic hermits, and martial arts practitioners. It is also important to note that advancement into the Dai Zhou Tian (Big Circle) will not happen without the initial attainment of the Xiao Zhou Tian (Small Circle). Of course, many factors need to be considered. Success in achieving the latter or both of these phenomena is still dependent on one's mental state, personality, benevolence, and wisdom. Furthermore, one's age, lifestyle, diet, lineage, training methods, length of training, perseverance, dedication, etc. are also all important factors in advancing to the phenomena of Dai Zhou Tian.

BIG CIRCLE (大周天)

Dai Zhou Tian, or Big Circle, occurs when Qi travels smoothly, without too many obstacles/blockages, in the following Meridian channels:

Lung Meridian of hand – Taiyin
Large intestine Meridian of hand – Yangming
Stomach Meridian of foot – Yangming
Spleen Meridian of foot – Taiyin
Heart Meridian of hand – Shaoyin
Small intestine Meridian of hand – Taiyang
Bladder Meridian of foot – Taiyang
Kidney Meridian of foot – Shaoyin
Pericardium Meridian of hand – Jueyin
Triple energizer Meridian of hand – Shaoyang
Gallbladder Meridian of foot – Shaoyang
Liver Meridian of foot – Jueyin

Again, from personal experience, Dai Zhou Tian can only be achieved after Qi travels smoothly and consistently in the Xiao Zhou Tian for a long period of time. In my case, it took approximately five additional years of diligent practice after experiencing the Xiao Zhou Tian, before finally advancing into the Dai Zhou Tian phase. Basically, Dai Zhou Tian is a condition in which the Qi travels from the bottom of your feet (Yongquan acupoint)

Dai Zhou Tian Diagram

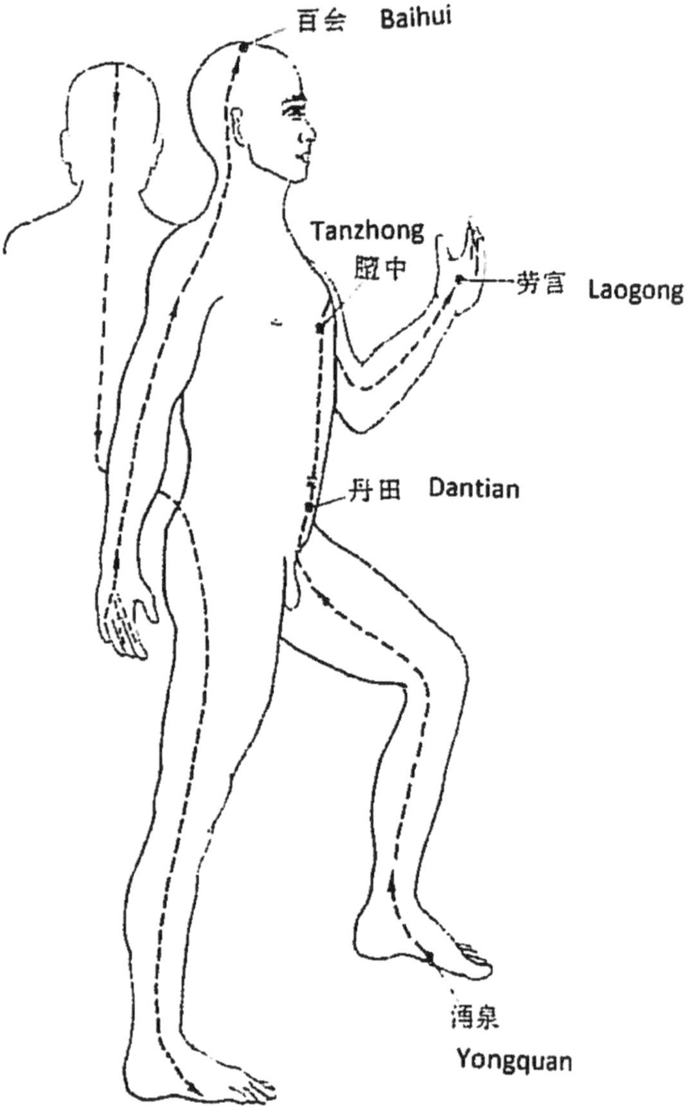

upward along the side, inside, and front of your legs to the Huiyin (midway between the anus and scrotum), before connecting with the Ren Meridian (Conception Vessel). From there, the Qi continues to travel further up to the face and eventually into the eyes. Some can even feel it traveling along their ears. For me, it took some additional time before the Qi traveled along the hands, and eventually to the finger tips (where it is possible to start projecting it outside the body).

I discussed some details regarding my progress with the Xiao Zhou Tian and Dai Zhou Tian in my 2009 Chinese book, "The Relationship of Tai Chi & Qi Emission" ("太極拳與布氣之妙合"), published in Hong Kong. The attainment of the Xiao Zhou Tian and Dai Zhou Tian are strong foundations for advanced levels in Qi projection. I must stress that almost everybody is able to emit Qi to some extent. However, the volume and intensity of the Qi emitted are dependent on the accumulation of it in your body. The more Qi accumulated in your Dantian, the greater your ammunition in preparing yourself for Qi projection. Without the accumulation of sufficient Qi, techniques used for Qi projection are only funny hand gestures, devoid of any healing effects. Hence, many are weary of the idea that Qi projection can be used for healing purposes. How can one tell whether Qi is truly being projected? Undoubtedly, there are people who claim to have the ability to project Qi despite only being able to do so weakly or not at all. In these cases, implications for healing purposes seem very insignificant. True Qi emission, with the potential for healing, is extremely strong and intense to the point where you can feel the energy penetrating your body. Without much strength, projected Qi would not be able to clear blockages within the body. Generally, only practitioners who have attained and perfected both the Xiao Zhou Tian *and* the Dai Zhou Tian will be able to emit a relatively high volume of Qi during projection.

MY TESTIMONY, BY SUE LEE

At the lowest point in my life, I had the opportunity to learn Qigong and Tai Chi from Sifu Kelly Kwan. This truly improved my health and changed my life completely.

In 2003, I found out from my annual medical check-up that my white blood cell count was extremely low. The normal level is approximately 4.0 but mine only read 1.7. I was referred to a cancer specialist, but despite numerous tests they could not find the cause of my problem. The specialist just told me to "Enjoy your life!" which to me, meant that mine would likely be short. He also advised that I should avoid staying in crowded places because of my relatively weak immune system. My immune system was so weak that if someone sneezed beside me, I would return home with a high fever. A single sneeze could force me to rest; bedridden for at least a week before seeing any signs of recovery.

One day, I had had enough. I said to myself that I needed to find a solution to fix my problem. Over time, I had noticed that my husband seemed more youthful and healthy than he did in years past. He had been studying Qigong and Tai Chi from Sifu Kelly for two years. I kept thinking that there must be a connection. In a mere two years, I had noticed a difference in my husband! Though hesitant, I decided to give Qigong and Tai Chi a try. After all, it was a better alternative than sitting at home and doing nothing!

After training with Sifu Kelly for about a year, I had another blood test. I really feared that I would have to go through the process of tedious testing again. The results indicated that my white blood cell count went up from 1.7 to 3.4. My specialist asked me what I did to yield such drastic improvements without taking any medication at all. I replied to him that all I did was practice Qigong and Tai Chi daily. He then repeatedly said "very good." My file was finally closed after a couple more visits. All the testing indicated a very positive result.

This was not the only time that I saw the effects of Qi first hand. In 2007, I injured my back by lifting a heavy box in the office. I rested at home and my family doctor suggested that I go see a physiotherapist. I went for quite a few sessions, but the treatment seemed to provide very little relief for my painful symptoms. I still had consistent pain all over my back. I was especially worried since I had already planned a trip overseas to Taiwan. My doctor told me I should not be taking a long flight because of my back. I told Sifu Kelly and he reassured me, telling me not to worry so much and that he would try and fix my problem. He then told me to relax and lie down on top of some gym mats. He put his hand over my back. All of a sudden, after about a minute or two, I felt like someone had made a hole in my back and all the pain was suddenly released from there. It was such an amazing sensation and experience. I still remember my boss asking me why I suddenly recovered so quickly. I just told her I had received a "secret treatment" from somebody, without explaining any of the details. I had a feeling something so amazing would be hard for others to believe.

I had another incident in July of 2013. I fell at home and fractured my left pinky toe. Unfortunately, my toe was broken into three sections. I was referred to a fracture clinic, but traditional medical treatment had provided very little help to improve my condition. Walking became difficult because I could hardly move or flex my toe due to excruciating pain. Forced to use a cane, my limited mobility made me feel quite depressed. Once again, I received Qi treatment from Sifu Kelly. I rested on a mat and Sifu was scanning my body from head to toe by moving his hands back and forth. He did not touch any part of my body at all and both his hands were just floating at least six inches or more above me. After a couple of minutes, I was suddenly jumping up and down, followed by seven consecutive sit-ups (something that I couldn't do even if I was not injured). I felt like I was being lifted by a fishing hook and my feet were moving and turning at a speed that most people could probably not imagine. All my pain was gone after a total of four treatments.

After all these years with Sifu Kelly, I have witnessed extraordinary advancement in terms of his skills and his Qi energy. Together with a couple of other students in his Tai Chi class, I can clearly see the Qi energy travel in different parts of his body when he is doing meditation with us.

I am not trying to convince others to believe in Qigong. Instead, I would just like to take this opportunity to document some of my own experiences with my Sifu and his Qi. I think it is just a matter of "seeing is believing."

ANOTHER WORLD, BY CHRISTINA WOLLESEN

Since I started training with Sifu Kelly about two years ago, Tai Chi has profoundly changed and deepened every single aspect of my life. I am more rooted physically, mentally, and spiritually, and feel more connected to my life's path than ever before.

There is no way I can expect anyone reading this to believe the things I have witnessed Sifu do with his energy: literally making people– often people with limited mobility, sometimes senior citizens– bounce off the ground, vigorously flail their limbs, and dance on the spot with no signs of physical exertion. After a few of these treatments, they would report that their symptoms of pain or illness were reduced or gone completely. I cannot expect you to believe these things, because I myself did not believe when I first heard about them. So, let me tell my own personal story.

I began Tai Chi in university. I would go to Sifu Kelly's class once a week after my mother had recommended it to me. She had been going for a few years, and would tell me incredible (literally, not credible) stories about the things he could do by "projecting his Qi". I was skeptical, but my mom, a holistic practitioner and martial artist with a black belt in Karate, insisted I should check it out.

The first time I was aware that something beyond just

physical exercise was happening was about eight months into my training. Towards the end of one of these classes, Sifu Kelly told me to stand still. He placed his hands near my stomach without touching me. I had seen him do this to other students, and witnessed their intense reactions. Sometimes they would appear to lose control of their bodies completely, spinning around the room in a circle. I did not spin, or flail, and this experience is not so memorable by virtue of its intensity. Rather, it is so unforgettable simply because I had never felt anything like that before. A door had been opened to another world. The experience lay outside the realm of my five senses, and I am still not sure how to intellectualize the part of my physical body that is now able to sense and receive this energy regularly (and to be honest, I have little desire or need to do so).

From there, I became more aware of the potential energy that can be accessed through Tai Chi. The next turning point in my practice came in 2013, when my father died suddenly of a heart attack. It destroyed me: I lost weight, spent weeks in bed, and developed a migraine that lasted over a month. I tried every kind of prescription painkiller to combat the headaches, but nothing worked. I only felt more nauseous, and the pain intensified. After several doctor visits, I went to Sifu Kelly for help. He gave me Qi projections and a set of Qigong exercises to do each day. Incredibly, my physical pain lessened. When Sifu projected his Qi into me, I would feel my body expelling – almost vomiting– something vast from inside of me. It was as if Sifu was drawing out a well of spiritual pain and releasing blockages — ones that ran far deeper than the death of my father.

This experience changed my practice entirely. I began doing the exercises regularly, and taking every opportunity to learn more about Tai Chi. The impact on my health has been immense. My insomnia is gone, and I do not need to rely on alcohol to relax my mind. Most incredibly, I don't get headaches anymore. My body is stronger than ever. Each day of practice brings a greater sense of fullness, and new discoveries.

A quick note before I go on: nothing about this account, or the others in this book is necessarily incompatible with a scientific perspective. The complexity and variables at play during a Qi projection (two unique living organisms interacting on a level that technology still cannot completely capture) are outside the standard Western framework for verifying the efficacy of a medical treatment. Yes, traditional science tells us that good experiments are replicable, but everything about projecting Qi is based on constant flux that defies this. But this does not mean that

Western science and Tai Chi are exclusive to one another. In fact, numerous studies show us that meditation, including Tai Chi and Qigong, has a significant impact on our brains and bodies. We have a lot to gain by keeping an open mind.

What I love about Tai Chi and Qigong (from here on, I will use Tai Chi to refer to both), is the fact that they are inherently movement based: our living bodies are essential to the process. Implicit in this is an acknowledgement of ourselves as inherently embodied, and the mind and body as being necessarily intertwined. This is so special, because a substantial part of the Western philosophical tradition is based on how the mind (an immaterial thing) can possibly be connected to the body (a material thing). The classic question encountered by first year philosophy students is, "How can we be sure we are not brains in vats?" But in Tai Chi, the very idea that the movement of our body stimulates the flow of our Qi posits that the material part of ourselves necessarily impacts the immaterial part. We develop relative to how we occupy and move in the space we are in, and cannot arbitrarily separate our minds from our bodies. In fact, contemporary philosophers of the mind are turning to Eastern Traditions (including Tai Chi) for more holistic portraits of the relationship between our minds and bodies. This makes sense: in Ancient Chinese, a single word that can roughly be translated as 'heart / mind' was used to describe the system which the Western tradition later separated into the mind and the body. Modern science is also in agreement, with some scientists arguing that the nerve endings in our fingers have as much to do with our mind as the grey matter in our head.

Beyond the philosophy of Tai Chi, I am moved by the ethereal realizations that come through practicing it. Qi is truly everywhere: from the energy that Sifu projects into others, to the Qi that exists inside us all, to the Qi of the universe– simultaneously different and the same, like infinite ocean waves. Every movement in the Tai Chi form is based on Yin and Yang, opening and closing, empty and full. Picture another realm where you are conscious that every motion of your being is a microcosm of the universe: death and rebirth, being and not being, all rising and falling and spilling over one another and filling you with profound bliss.

At my best as an artist, I feel I am floating above the work, connecting to something beyond myself and channeling something simple and pure. That purity, or clarity, is important to me because I believe it is what allows a work to resonate, and allows an audience to be moved. Tai Chi has given me the gift, albeit for a moment, to begin to control that clarity within myself. To step outside of time, and to touch that (sometimes scary) limitless thing that knows no confines. A reminder of the existence of this space, and to be able to connect to it sometimes, is the most beautiful gift.

As much I try to communicate the experience of practicing Tai Chi, I can never capture it fully using words alone. In the Chinese Book of Changes by Lao Tzu, he compares our words to a fisherman's net: useful only to catch and hold the fish (or concept), after which it can be discarded. Do the same with the words I've written here, which are nothing more than a rough sketch of my own experience. Tai Chi and Qigong, like all things of value, must be learned through live discourse and *practice.* I am forever indebted to Sifu Kelly for taking the time to pass on some of his wisdom to me. He has taught me all I know about Tai Chi. He opened a door for me into another world, and in walking me through he has forever changed my life.

QI PROJECTION IN HEALING

Qigong healing or "energy healing" originated in China more than 2000 years ago. As previously mentioned, the treatment should only be performed by more advanced Qigong practitioners. Through methods such as Qi cultivation, diligent practice, and Qi projection, the internal Qi within a practitioner travels throughout their entire body, circulating in a fashion which facilitates projection for treatment purposes. With certain techniques, emission of Qi will pass through the Meridian system of the patient. Thus, specific acupoints and the surrounding tissues may be targeted to treat certain ailments– even those that are isolated and localized to a certain area.

According to the Chinese medicinal point of view, patients experience symptoms of pain due to blockages in their system. Projecting Qi will stimulate and activate the patient's own internal Qi, relieving their blockages while harmonizing Yin and Yang to adjust the balance and function of the internal organs. Those who are weak will be strengthened and those who are tense will experience relief (lowering pressure within the body). Chinese medicine also believes that Qi therapy can boost the immune system to improve overall health. Treatment proves to be most effective for hormone imbalance, insomnia, anxiety, and especially chronic pains (e.g. frozen shoulder, arthritis, headaches/migraines, stomach problems, muscle pains and tension, sciatica, etc.).

Each individual's response to energy projection will be different. Some may have more obvious reactions such as vigorous and spontaneous movements (e.g. spinning, flipping, shaking, tapping, or beating different parts of their body), while others may only experience a mild sensation such as static or heat. The patient's own energy field is directly related to their sensitivity (i.e. patients who practice Qigong themselves or consistently do meditation tend to exhibit greater sensitivity). Also, practising Qigong together with an advanced level master will enhance the surrounding Qi field and thus, improve the overall sensitivity of the practitioners during the reception of Qi. Females tend to be more sensitive than males in their reactions to Qi projection. I have seen this time and time again in my students and patients.

It is important to note that Qi projection needs a great degree of cooperation from the patients in order to achieve good results. It is especially crucial for patients to relax themselves fully, both physically and mentally, before the emitted external Qi can fully travel into their Meridian channels and acupoints. Once this occurs, the Qi activates and combines with the internal Qi of the patient, traveling along the Meridian channels and helping to clear their blockages. In general, Qi projection will not work if the patient chooses to block off the emitted Qi, either intentionally or unintentionally, by refusing to relax themselves fully (both physically and mentally). The environment and setting in which Qi healing is performed is also very important. Normally, quiet, private, and relaxed settings (free of any interruptions or distractions) are necessary for better results in Qi healing. The physical and mental condition of the master is also vital for the quality and quantity of Qi projected. Qi projection will be hindered for those who adopt a negative or challenging attitude or mood. Moreover, both patients and masters need to have confidence and belief in the treatment in order to see its true benefits.

I must emphasize that Qi healing takes time, and to achieve lasting or permanent results, one session is usually not enough. In order to see consistent results, the normal course of treatment must last for at least 8 sessions (1 session/week), depending on the severity of the condition being treated. Usually, Phase I of my Qi healing treatment will include 10 minutes of initial meditation with the patient to encourage Qi cultivation within their body (either in a relaxed sitting or standing position). This process serves to establish the energy field necessary for the reception of Qi when it is projected and transmitted to the patient during the second phase of treatment. The initial meditation phase is crucial in order to heighten the sensitivity of the patient to the Qi healing. Phase II will include about 10 minutes of intensive Qi therapy where Qi is projected either throughout the body or concentrated on the target area. The final 15 minutes of treatment will be a short lesson on take-home exercises to help strengthen and maintain one's energy level. This will influence the reception of Qi and the circulation of Qi within the body.

LING KONG JING

Ling Kong Jing or Empty Force normally refers to a phenomenon in which certain exceptionally high-level Tai Chi masters are able to manipulate Qi in push hands or fighting situations. In some cases, they are able to make their opponents stumble, bounce backwards, and/or fall over with or without touching them.

Ling Kong Jing is effective mostly in push hands practice between a student and master. Students are more easily able to relax themselves while doing push hands with their masters. This promotes a more receptive mode and provides a better condition for the master to manipulate his external Qi. An interruption of the regular flow of Qi within the student's Meridian channels and system is the result. However, Ling Kong Jing by itself is not that effective in fighting situations since the opponent is often engaged in an aggressive state of mind. Their mind and body become quite rigid. Thus, the emitted external Qi cannot fully enter into the opponent's Meridian channels.

The effectiveness of Ling Kong Jing in application is highly dependent on one's practical skills, previous training, and combat experience. Ling Kong Jing, combined with exceptional skills, will definitely enhance one's ability in push hands or in real life combat situations.

DEVELOPING QI PROJECTION TECHNIQUES

There are many techniques in regards to Qi projection. In the past and even nowadays, many of these techniques were kept secret and passed on only to gatekeepers, in-door disciples, or chosen few of the family. This is the major reason why many of these techniques are still kept secret among the Tao or Zen families.

Qi Projection Diagram

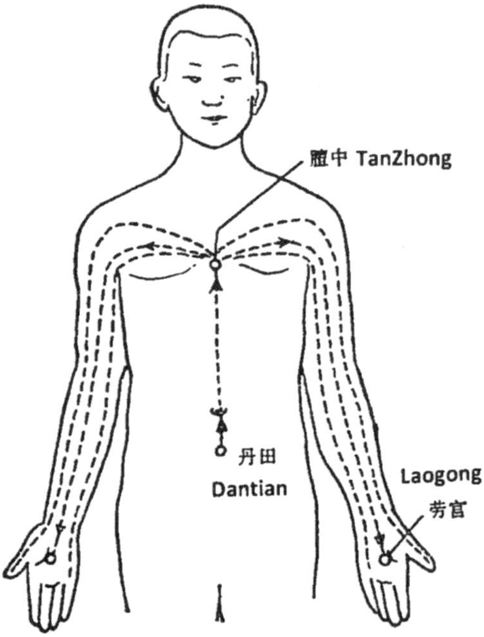

In my view, one very efficient technique for Qi projection is developed through Zhan Zhuang (standing meditation) training, which can be used to cultivate your internal Qi over a period of time. With the imagination (intent) of drawing Qi from the universe through Baihui (crown of your head) into your body, along with the combination of the Qi generated from the Dantian, you can focus your mind and concentrate on your Dantian. Then, using your mind, you can lead your Qi up to your Tanzhong (midway between the nipples) and allow it to travel up to your shoulders, to the inner part of your arm, and finally out through the Laogong in your palm (a point between the 2nd and 3rd metacarpal bones, where the tip of the middle finger touches when the fist is clenched). Other techniques include making different hand gestures (i.e. Sword Fingers) and /or combining the chanting of different sounds in order to activate the Qi in the various organs of your body. More advanced techniques include the projection of Qi through the Baihui (crown of your head), Yintang (the midpoint of the medial ends of the eyebrows), the eyes, the ears, or using only the mind.

Some specific training methods require a very solid foundation. This rings true especially for methods such as "Iron Shirt," "Iron Stomach," "Iron Groin," or other hard Qigong training. In the past, most of these techniques were taught only to selected disciples who were young. Such training in their early years meant flexibility and malleability that could help to achieve a better result.

It is known that people with a mild degree of anxiety, insomnia, or depression seem to be better off practicing Tai Chi or other moving meditation exercises instead. The element of movement allows practitioners to focus more on the structure of the movements instead of utilizing too much intent in the mind. In general, this is also a very effective way for students to develop a good natural flow of energy in their movements. In some cases, too much intent will lead to stagnation in terms of movements and Qi flow.

ZHAN ZHUANG

(站樁, STANDING MEDITATION)

Although Zhan Zhuang is a very effective training method for internal Qi cultivation, if not done correctly, it can also have many serious and harmful implications for one's health. The cause of these negative effects is mostly due to incorrect posture, usually in the way that one stands. Many Qigong practitioners try to connect "three points in one line" ("三點一線") during this stationary standing meditation. That is, imagining the Baihui (crown of the head), Huiyin (midway between the anus and the scrotum), and Yongquan (located on the sole, in the depression with foot in plantar flexion, approximately at the anterior third and the posterior two thirds of the line from the web between the 2nd and 3rd toes to the back of the heel) all being connected in their body. However, this tends to lead to the shifting of one's body weight to the front part of the feet in training. This habit will stimulate the Yongquan acupoints, giving an initial boost to the kidney and sex glands. It will then increase your libido. Most practitioners may find that initially, the function of their kidneys is strengthened. However, with time, the persistent pressure and stimulation of the Yongquan will also lead to high blood pressure. This is especially true for those who had relatively weak kidney function to begin with.

The body is sensitive, and balance is not an easy state to achieve in Qigong. This is one of the reasons why some Qigong masters experience serious strokes in later phases of their training. To avoid the negative implications associated with over-stimulation of the Yongquan, I suggest shifting one's body weight to the heel, instead of leaning forward during Zhan Zhuang. Again, it is critical to remember that Zhan Zhuang is not suitable for everyone and it is important to seek guidance from an experienced Qigong master if you intend on partaking in this type of training. One's diet, emotions, and habits are all significant factors related to the success of your training. Holistic lifestyles are extremely vital in enhancing your cultivation of Qi energy.

I must stress once more that strict and direct guidance from a knowledgeable master is strongly recommended while engaging in any serious Zhan Zhuang training.

ARE ALL QIGONG TRAINING METHODS SUITABLE FOR EVERYONE?

Much related to the previous chapter on Zhan Zhuang and its possible negative implications, some Qigong practitioners are advised not to engage in serious stationary Qigong training methods such as standing and sitting meditation. This is especially the case for those who have mental health conditions such as severe depression, schizophrenia, anxiety, phobias, or other hidden mental health issues. Engaging in such trainings with serious intent can further activate and worsen any underlying psychological problems. This is a condition we call "Qigong Psychosis" or "Kundalini Psychosis" ("走火入魔") which literally translates to being "burnt with fire and allowing demons to enter."

I strongly believe that a good and knowledgeable master should never arbitrarily impose training methods onto their students without first observing the mental state and condition of their students. This is a core value I have adopted in my teaching, and I feel that a responsible Sifu has the obligation to guide his or her students' training in a way that is safe, unique, and effective. That being said, each student learns in a different way, and it takes a true master to know how to best create a lesson plan that is suitable for each student's individual strengths and needs.

ELIMINATION OF THOUGHTS IN MEDITATION

It is true to say that all Qigong practitioners try to eliminate or empty most, if not all, of their "thoughts" during meditation. Many choose to focus their minds on breathing or visualizations. Some count the number of breaths that they take while others imagine beautiful scenic images such as a floating river or clouds. Another popular approach is to try and focus the intent on certain Meridian acupoints in the body during meditation. However, it is extremely difficult for most people to achieve such a goal.

After many years of meditation, my experience has taught me that there is no need to place all your concentration on how to empty your "thoughts" at all. Instead, let those "thoughts" co-exist with you in the meditation process. It is just like treating oneself as a separate small universe surrounded by a big universe that is the world around us. The small universe will fully integrate with the big universe slowly and gradually without interfering with or disturbing either world. In this way, the rhythm, frequency, and tempo of both universes will remain the same. Your mind will indeed be more calm and peaceful and you will enter into a state of harmony naturally. You no longer need to use any artificial effort in trying to empty the thoughts in your mind anymore. From this point, your Qi will flow naturally along your Meridian channels in your body as long as you can maintain your focus in relaxing yourself.

The idea behind meditation is to erase the boundaries between your own self and the world around you. In the process of fully relaxing your body and mind, it may be beneficial to “cushion” your thoughts. For example, you may imagine yourself standing or sitting in a cloud of cotton. By doing so, this should help your body feel weightless, as if you are a bubble floating in the air. Without any burdens, one can merge and integrate the self with the surrounding universe effortlessly.

太極拳
一九九二年

PART THREE

TAI CHI AND NEIGONG

IS TRADITIONAL TAI CHI A KIND OF QIGONG?

Many martial artists and Tai Chi practitioners will agree that Tai Chi is a type of martial arts training with tremendous health benefits. However, despite the common view that Tai Chi can also be classified as a type of "Neigong" (internal training), many refuse to accept the fact that Tai Chi is actually a part of Qigong.

The main source of confusion comes from the terminology. In the past, the term "Neigong" was widely used to refer to trainings such as "Yijinjing" and the "Golden Bell" trainings. These are the internal training exercises practiced by many martial art learners. Its functions are to strengthen the muscles, tendons, bones, sinews, and internal organs by using a wooden or iron mallet to repeatedly strike the surface of the body. The theory behind the training is that after repeating the exercises for a long time, the initial feelings of pain subside and leave your

Opposite page: Tai Chi Chuan calligraphy by my late father, Kwan Choi Man (關采文), 1992

body and back as strong as iron. Nowadays, people are still associating the aforementioned methods with "Iron Shirt," "Iron Groin," or even Tai Chi, Hsing Yi, and Pa Kua– referring to all of them collectively as "Neigong." Many martial artists are inclined to classify these martial arts training styles with the implication of Neigong instead of Qigong. The truth is, Neigong normally refers to a subset of specific training methods within the family of Qigong. This fact is supported by many famous Tai Chi Grandmasters such as Ma Yue Liang (馬岳樑, Wu family Tai Chi), Cheng Man Ching (鄭曼青), Wu Tu Nan (吳圖南), and Huang Xing Xiang (黃性賢); all of whom have openly stated (on many occasions) that Tai Chi is indeed a kind of Qigong.

Through my many years of training, I have come to realize that Tai Chi, together with certain internal training methods, will lead to a strong accumulation of Qi in the Dantian and eventually result in the attainment of the Xiao Zhou Tian (Small Circle) and possibly even the Dai Zhou Tian (Big Circle). Nearly all traditional families of Tai Chi (Chen, Yang, Wu, Hao, and Sun) have their own unique way of internal training to cultivate internal Qi energy.

In hindsight, I have found that Tai Chi practitioners who preoccupy their training with fighting applications without training in Qi cultivation will rarely develop great levels of Qi. In addition, combining Tai Chi training with other techniques such as boxing, wrestling, or other hard external martial arts will make it even more difficult to develop internal Qi. This is because a lot of one's internal energy will be exhausted, making it challenging to build up Qi in the body. Furthermore, adopting a fighting mentality means focusing on aggression and concentrating on a strategy to defeat your opponent. When the mind is preoccupied with these thoughts, engaging in internal training such as Zhan Zhuang (standing meditation) becomes nearly impossible as the mind cannot relax. At some point, you need to drop your "aggressiveness" completely in order for your mind to engage in any serious Qi cultivation training. Qi is not likely to develop if you have too much baggage or are preoccupied by your desires. A kind heart, benevolence, and wisdom will definitely reduce the obstacles you will come across during the journey to the centre of your mind.

NEIGONG

I had the opportunity to train in Neigong with Master Wong in 1998. This Neigong originated from the Wu family Tai Chi school. In the past, it was only transmitted within the family. Only a handful of indoor disciples had the privilege of learning these techniques. In fact, a complete set of this art is said to be lost in transmission in mainland China. My Sifu, Master Wong is one of the few masters who are knowledgeable about its details.

Master Wong told me he learned this Neigong first from Master Cheng Tin Hung (鄭天熊) in the 1960s and later from his Sifu, Grandmaster Wu Tai Chi (吳大齊, 4th generation Grandmaster of the Wu's family Tai Chi) in the 1970s. Moreover, he was able to gather more details from a Sifu, Chung Ngo Ping (鍾岳平). Sifu Chung was an indoor disciple of Grandmaster Wu Kung Yi (吳公儀, father of Wu Tai Chi). Master Wong told me that Sifu Chung was extremely loyal and dedicated most of his spare time to Grandmaster Wu Kung Yi. He always accompanied his Sifu everywhere and would not even leave his Sifu's side until he saw him resting in bed at night. It is because of this close relationship that he earned the privilege to learn most of the secret skills and techniques.

Master Wong befriended Sifu Chung when they both attended a class on Tui Na (Chinese massage) and acupuncture. According to my Sifu, Chung was a very skinny man and weighed only about 100lbs. He started to learn Tai Chi after suffering from tuberculosis during the late 1950s. However, he was extremely skillful in Tai Chi Push Hands in which he could easily unbalance a much stronger and bigger opponent. According to Master Wong, he witnessed Sifu Chung lift up the foot of a classmate without touching it by manipulating and projecting his Qi energy during a demo at one of their acupuncture classes. However, Sifu Chung did not practice any other Qigong besides Tai Chi. In fact, he spent most his life researching into the art of Tai Chi with Grandmaster Wu Kung Yi.

The aforementioned Neigong training is a set of different movements which should be practised daily. It combines both movements and stationary stances together with softness and Fa Jing (a term which means performing an action fast with explosive force) in training. Its function is to improve one's overall ability in terms of rooting (stronger stance), stamina, power (both internal and external), and endurance. This training is designed to allow the body to withstand any strong pounding forces from beating or punching. From my own experience, this type of training also has some shortcomings and side effects if practised incorrectly. It should be closely supervised, and guidance from an experienced master while training is crucial. In addition, one's age, physical condition, as well as diet and lifestyle are extremely important in determining the outcome of training.

Some famous masters who are popular with the training of this Neigong do and have suffered from diabetes, kidney disease, high blood pressure, strokes, and heart disease. In my view, these masters suffered from these illnesses not necessarily as a direct result of the training itself. I believe it is mostly associated with the excessive intensity of the training together with an improper lifestyle (e.g. daily diet, eating and drinking habits (alcoholism), and, in some cases, too much sexual practice before and after training).

HOLISTIC LIFESTYLE

According to Taoist doctrines and the ancient Chinese school on health and longevity, holistic lifestyles are comprised of a healthy diet, emotional management, and exercise such as martial arts and Qigong training.

A healthy diet is very important in maintaining health and longevity, as well as preventing disease. The daily intake of foods should emphasize natural organic meats, grains, and fresh fruits and vegetables. The percentage should be 30% meat and 70% mixed grains, vegetables, and fruits. Try to stay away from grilled, deep fried, greasy, and processed foods. Moderate drinking is fine, but smoking should be avoided completely.

The fluctuation of our emotions can have a very negative impact on the Qi flow, blood circulation, and overall function of the internal organs in our body. Excessive emotions are harmful to our health, both physically and mentally. Thus, it is very important to exercise control by harmonizing our "Seven Emotions" and "Six Desires." According to the Taoist school and traditional Chinese medicine, the "Seven Emotions" are joy, fear, anger, grief, worry, sentiments, and affection. The "Six Desires" are lust, vanity, dignity, pleasant sounds, good life, and sensual pleasures. It is very important for us to balance these emotions and desires through the daily intake of food, drink (soups and herbal medicines), sexual practice, martial arts, and Qigong training (both moving and stationary trainings). Normally, moderate sexual practice is good, but you need to have some discipline and control over it. The ancient school on health and longevity suggested some guidelines for people to follow. For example, one time in 7 days (if you are in your 20s), 14 days (30s), 28 days (40s), and 45 days (50s). This guideline is for reference only and varies for each person. It is important to regulate your sexual practice if you plan on advancing in martial arts or Qigong training.

Above all, Qigong practice is the most important and effective way to maintain good health and longevity by balancing the Yin and Yang in our body. Such training also helps to promote a good balance of the mind, body, and soul in a natural way.

ABOUT THE AUTHOR

Sifu Kelly Kwan (關懷寬師傅) was born and raised in Hong Kong, and received his university education in Canada. He currently works as a social worker and department coordinator at a local community centre.

He has been practicing Yang Style Tai Chi and Qigong since 1984 in Hong Kong. After immigrating to Canada, he met one of the top masters in Chinese martial arts, Grandmaster Pan Qing Fu. In 1990, he became Grandmaster Pan's first formal disciple in Canada. He later met another Qigong master, Tai Yeen Wong, with whom he studied Qigong and Wu style Tai chi for about 10 years.

Sifu Kelly Kwan has been teaching Tai Chi and Qigong (both group and private lessons) in his spare time for over 25 years. In 2007, he developed his ability in Qi projection after ongoing intensive training for 23 consecutive years. He is known for his Qi energy healing. In 2009, Sifu Kelly Kwan published his first book, "The Relationship of Tai Chi and Qi Emission" ("太極拳與布氣之妙合") with his brother, Kwan Wai Kwong (關懷廣) in Hong Kong.

Outside of Qigong, Sifu Kelly Kwan has a profound love for nature and is especially attracted to large trees, mountains, rivers, and oceans. He also enjoys high quality Chinese tea and natural organic foods. He collects Yixing purple clay teapots, old bonsai trees, and Chinese calligraphy, paintings, and books. He is also one of few collectors with a large assortment of rare and old Chinese martial arts books.

51087894R00059

Made in the USA
Charleston, SC
10 January 2016